OVER 300 VISUAL VERBAL PUZZLES

(hand in hand)

(say when)

(too close for comfort)

(first rate)

(for the birds)

(it crossed my mind)

MindWare®
brainy toys for kids of all ages®

www.MINDWAREonline.com

A MindWare® Original!

Our entire selection of Brainy Toys for Kids of All Ages® is available at www.MINDWAREonline.com, or by calling us at 800-999-0398 to request a catalog.

Coloring Books

Each of our coloring books offer one of a kind patterns, textures and styles you make your own by choosing how to bring them to life.

Animal Habitats Series

Creature Camouflage Series

Designs Series

Lights Series

Modern Patterns Series

Mosaics Series

Quilts Series

Scapes Series

Transformations Series

Puzzle Books

Our puzzle books build skills in many areas—from logic to math, spatial reasoning to verbal skills.

Addition Adventures

Analogy Challenges

Clip Clue Puzzles

Code Breakers

Decimal Destinations

Deducibles

Directive Detective

Division Designs

Fast Fact Trivia

Fraction Finders

Grid Perplexors

Logic Links

Math Path Puzzles

Math Perplexors

More Multiplication Mosaics

Multiplication Mosaics

Noodlers

Number Circuits

Number Junctions

Perplexors

Sequencers

Subtraction Secrets

Tactic Twisters

Tan-Tastic Tangrams

Venn Perplexors

Word Winks

Word Wise

Games and Activities

Building blocks to strategic games, mystery puzzles to imaginative play — enhance abstract thinking and reasoning skills with our ingenious games and activities.

Bella's Mystery Decks

Blik-Blok

Block Buddies

Chaos

Cross-Eyed

Flip 4

Gambit

Hue Knew?

Logic Links Game

Make Your Own Mask Kit

Noodlers Game

Pattern Play

Qwirkle

Tally Rally

Squzzles

Configure nine 3 x 3 pieces into a square where all images match up on every single side. Three challenging puzzles per box.

3-D Scramblers

Animal Babies

Botanicals

Creature Kingdom

Creepy Crawlers

Dinosaurs!

Illusions

Insect Infested

Nocturnal Animals

Optical Illusions

Play Ball!

Wings & Wheels

World Money

© 2004 MindWare Holdings, Inc.

Illustrations by Tess Zimmer

All rights reserved. Printed in the U.S.A.

Limited reproduction permission. The publisher grants permission to reproduce up to 100 copies of any part of this book for noncommercial classroom or individual use. Any further duplication is prohibited.

EAN 978-1-892069-75-7
SKU 25067

for other MindWare products visit our website
www.MINDWAREonline.com

steven = steven

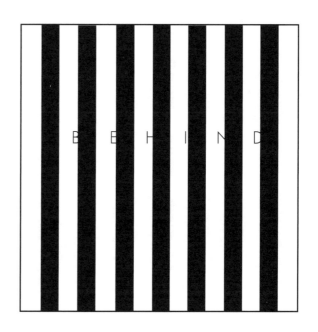

© 2004 MindWare®

3

PRIORITY

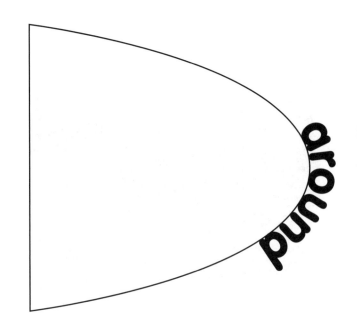

SET

GRAB
GRAB
GRAB
GRAB

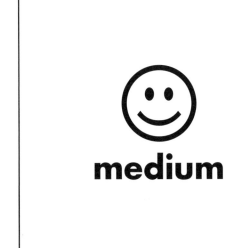

medium

4

© 2004 MindWare®

HhAaNnDd

word
word
word
word
word

© 2004 MindWare®

SECON D

TIMING

gear

1 RATE

SHEEP
WOLF
CLOTHING

GUT
GUT GUT
GUT GUT GUT
GUT GUT GUT
GUT GUT GUT GUT

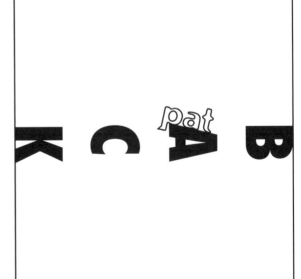

K C pat A B

6

© 2004 MindWare®

 YEAR ◯

 ROLL PUNCH PUNCH

HOLD

kill
σne

your SKIN
_____

 TE|ETH LIFE T|EETH

© 2004 MindWare®

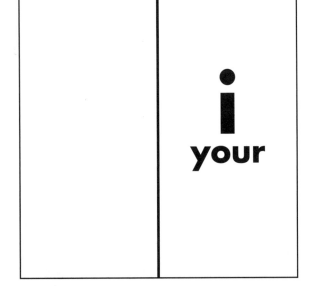

© 2004 MindWare®

spring MIND MIND

CUFF

DUTY
DUTY

time, time

beat beat beat beat beat beat beat beat beat beat beat beat beat beat BUSH

BRAKE
BRAKE

© 2004 MindWare®

TOUGH

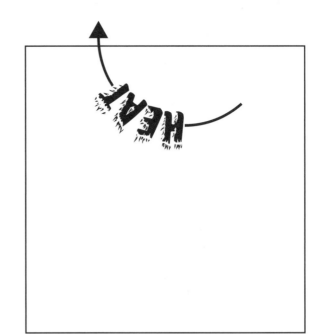

feed

**RAIN, SNOW
SLEET, HAIL
FOG, SUNSHINE
HUMID, BREEZY
CLOUDY**

feeling

STICK

REASON with

© 2004 MindWare®

iNSiDE

old 🕐
old 🕐
old 🕐
old 🕐

SAKE

SCRATCH
SCRATCH

HEAD

POCKET
POCKET

1
2
3
4
5

NONE
NONE

© 2004 MindWare®

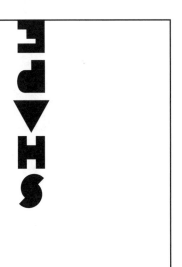

© 2004 MindWare®

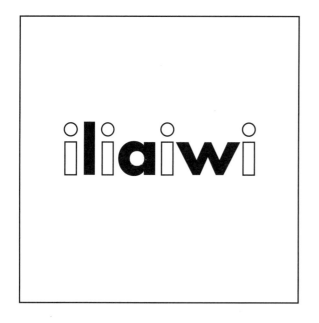

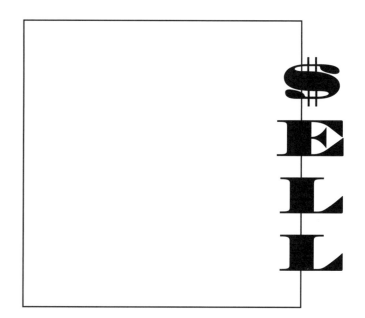

© 2004 MindWare®

----
same page

TOUGH
NUT
2

toe _____

© 2004 MindWare®

H●LE

rake
COALCOAL

par
par
par
par

COURSE

TIME

TRIP

1

© 2004 MindWare®

See eye to eye

YOUR ALLEY

Up your alley

LIFE

Life in the palm of your hands

MU~STARD

Cut the mustard

HAY
NEEDLE HAY
HAY
HAY
HAY

Needle in a haystack

INSULT
+
INJURY

Add insult to injury

16

© 2004 MindWare®

heaven
heaven
heaven
heaven
heaven
heaven
✹✹ heaven ✹✹

TIME = $

share

AND

share

HANGING

```
C   C   C
A   A   A
U   U   U
G   G   G
H   H   H
T   T   T
```

© 2004 MindWare®

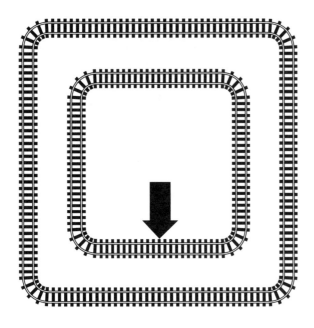

18

© 2004 MindWare®

© 2004 MindWare®

ARM ARM

G N I RTSSTR I N G

headHEADHEAD

20

© 2004 MindWare®

eyebrow

eyebrow

eyebrow

eyebrow eyebrow eyebrow
eyebrow eyebrow eyebrow
eyebrow eyebrow eyebrow

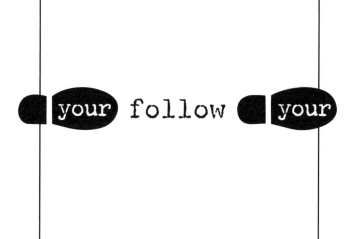

your follow your

WAGON
WAGON
WAGON

WEAR
LONG

© 2004 MindWare®

THINK+

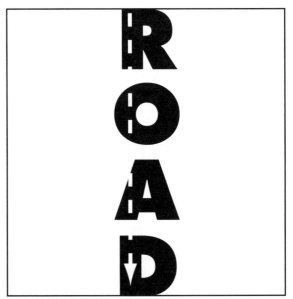

© 2004 MindWare®

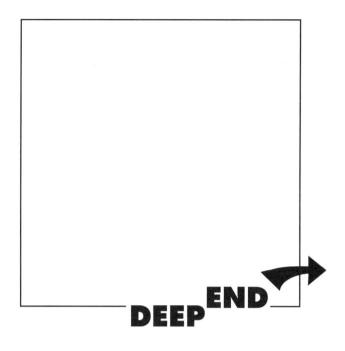

DEEP END →

NICK

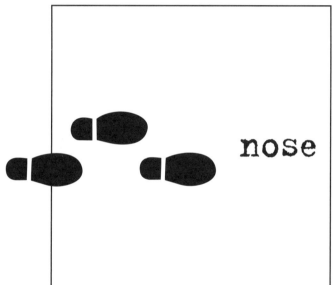

nose

haha ... *HO HO* ... hee hee ...
haha ... *HO HO* ... hee hee ...
haha ... *HO HO* ... hee hee ...
haha ... *HO HO* ... hee hee ...
haha ... *HO HO* ... hee hee ...
haha ... *HO HO* ... hee hee ...
haha ... *HO HO* ... hee hee ...
haha ... *HO HO* ...BANK

GRAVE

WINDING

© 2004 MindWare®

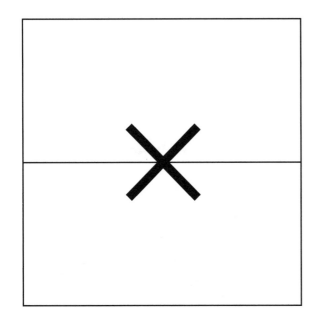

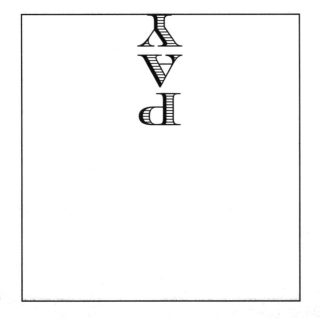

24

© 2004 MindWare®

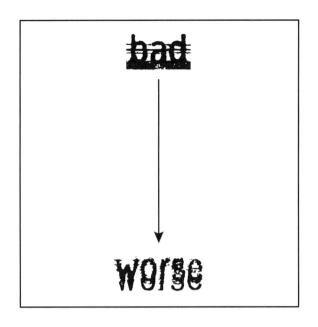

nOeUcCkH!

© 2004 MindWare®

imallgination

EAR EAR

THE

26

© 2004 MindWare®

 GET

I've had it

 YOUR

INFLUENCE

 HOG

© 2004 MindWare®

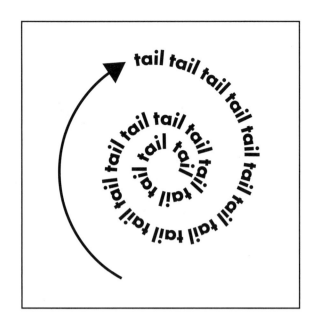

Running EMPTY

swear

𝕭ible
𝕭ible
𝕭ible
𝕭ible

© 2004 MindWare®

bbbbbbb

Practice   Practice

Practice

Practice

Practice

© 2004 MindWare®

EXPERIENCE

A ^{U} I ^{P} R

L
E
F
T
F
I
E
L
D

his HEAD

ado ado ado ado
ado ado ado
ado ado ado ado
NOTHING
ado ado ado ado
ado ado ado
ado ado ado ado

handle
SITUATION

© 2004 MindWare®

© 2004 MindWare®

HAVE it *This Way*

HAVE it That Way

best **FOOT**

once

12:38

chicken

MAN
—————————
BOARD

NO NO NO NO NO NO NO NO NO NO NO NO NO NO

© 2004 MindWare®

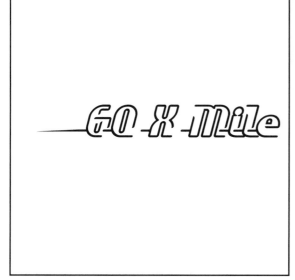

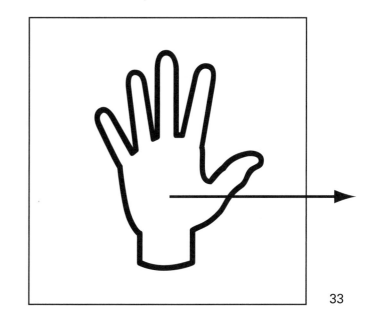

© 2004 MindWare®

CRUST

MONTH

sunday sunday sunday
sunday sunday sunday
sunday sunday sunday
sunday sunday sunday
sunday sunday sunday
sunday sunday sunday

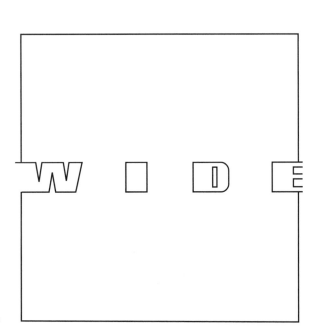

34

© 2004 MindWare®

it **BEST**
BEST
BEST
BEST

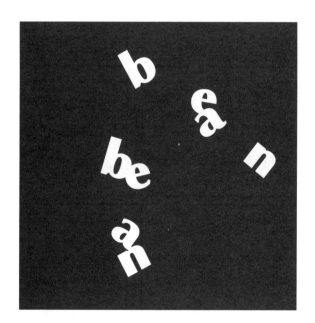

your HAND

© 2004 MindWare®

TIDE

2TO

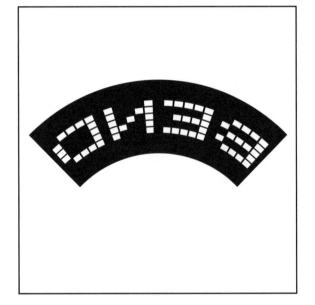

1,2,3,4,5,6
ME

HOT

FALL

PRESS

© 2004 MindWare®

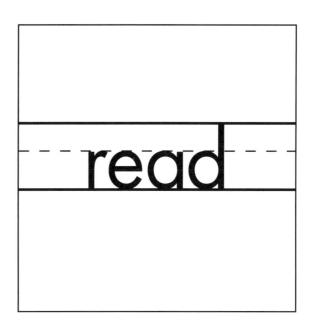

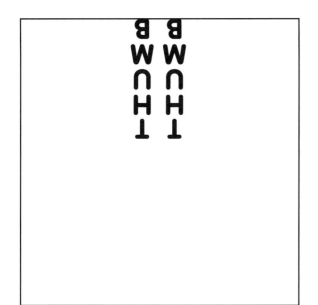

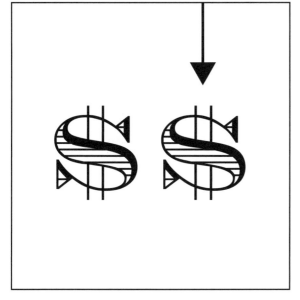

the end.

© 2004 MindWare®

LEAF
LEAF
LEAF
LEAF
LEAF
LEAF
LEAF

s.s.same

L
O O
O O
K
HIM

your MIND IN

WILL
WAY

BELT

© 2004 MindWare®

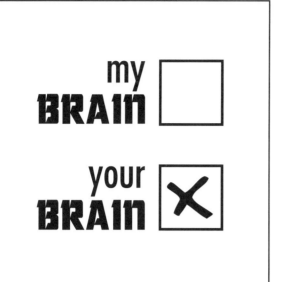

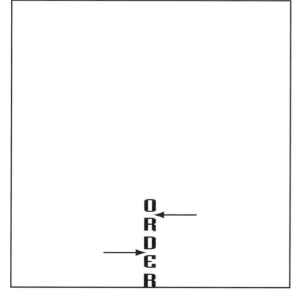

© 2004 MindWare®

STRAW
STRAW
STRAW
STRAW
→ STRAW ←

COME

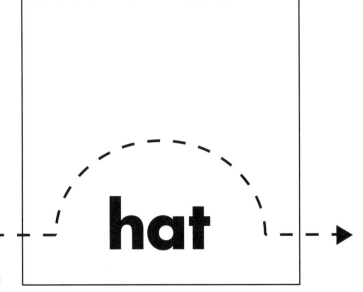

40

© 2004 MindWare®

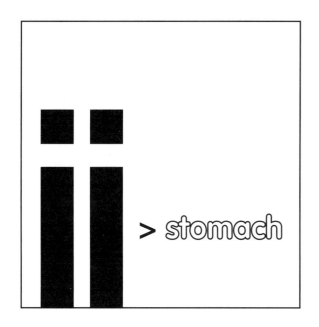

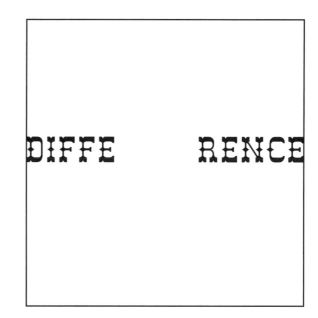

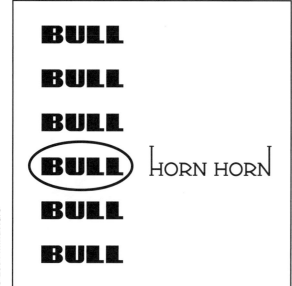

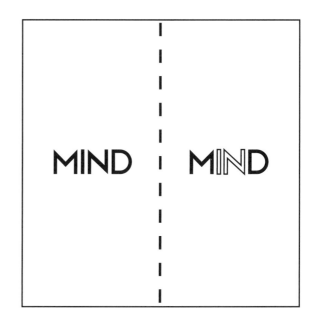

© 2004 MindWare®

string string string string

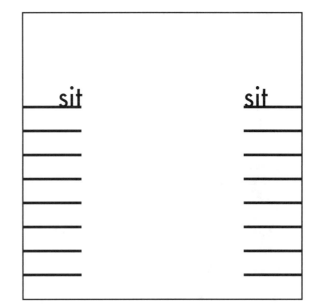

sit   sit

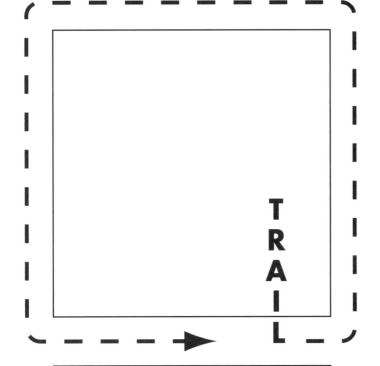

TRAIL

WORLD

FRONT

coin

BACK

coin

© 2004 MindWare®

© 2004 MindWare®

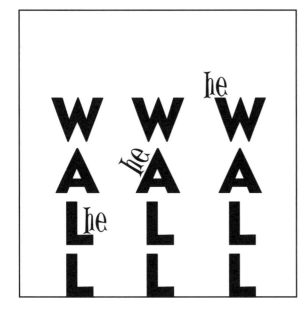

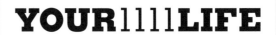

© 2004 MindWare®

© 2004 MindWare®

1   dozen
1   dozen
1   dozen
1   dozen
1   dozen
1   dozen

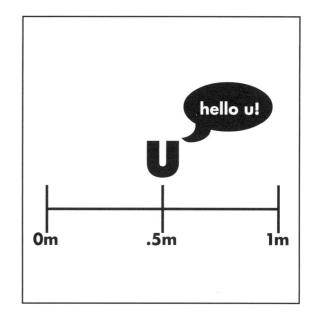

MIND

HEAVEN = HEAVEN

a w a k e

DAY
DAY
DAY
DAY
end

RUNNING neck
neck

HAND
HAND

hello MIND HI MIND

CHANCE
―――
2

© 2004 MindWare®

CONSCIENCE

STEP

ear

S
T
R
E
A
M

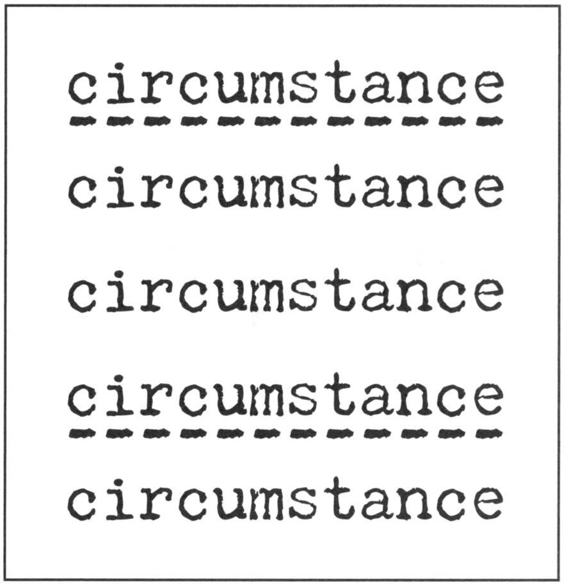
circumstance
circumstance
circumstance
circumstance
circumstance

© 2004 MindWare®

SURFACE

Welcome WEAR

MARK →

SHAPE GET IT

CONTROL everything

© 2004 MindWare®

my back

u

day day

SHOUL**DER** chip

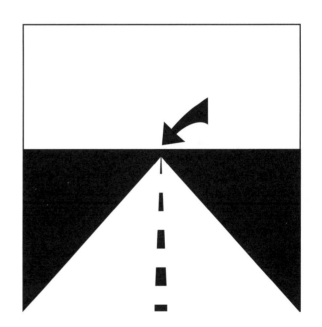

B
A
C
K

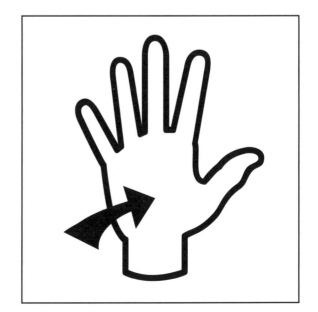

© 2004 MindWare®

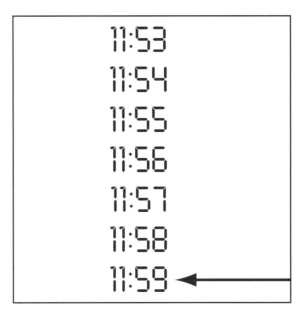

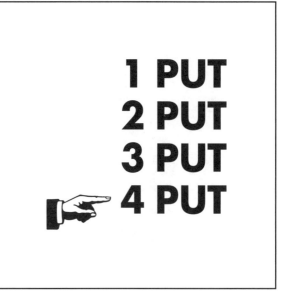

© 2004 MindWare®

my

BROKE

OPEN
&
BOARD

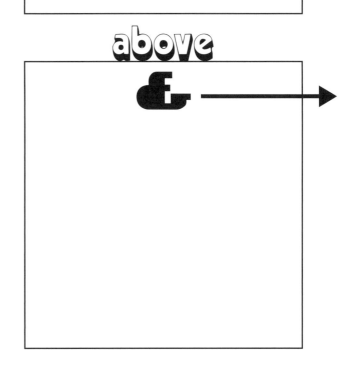

above
&

11 25 39
13 27 41
15 29 43
17 31 45
19 33 47 US
21 35 49
23 37 51

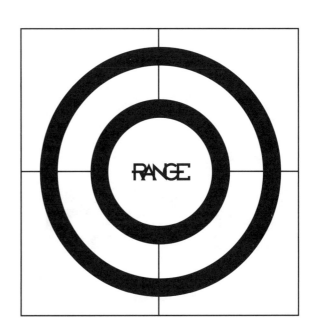

RANGE

© 2004 MindWare®

CART,

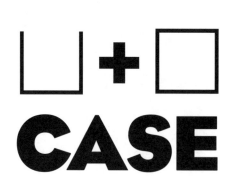

CASE

1 blessing
2 blessing
3 blessing
4 blessing

H2O

© 2004 MindWare®

PUZZLE ANSWERS pages 3 – 16

page 3
1. break the ice
2. even steven
3. race against the clock
4. for the birds
5. too close for comfort
6. behind bars

page 4
1. high priority
2. around the bend
3. set back
4. up for grabs
5. shaken up
6. happy medium

page 5
1. first and ten
2. forgive and forget
3. out in the open
4. hand in hand
5. the last word
6. ants in your pants

page 6
1. split second timing
2. first rate
3. high gear
4. a wolf in sheep's clothing
5. spill your guts
6. pat on the back

page 7
1. year round
2. roll with the punches
3. holdup
4. kill two birds with one stone
5. under your skin
6. lie through your teeth

page 8
1. shake down
2. stab in the back
3. around the clock
4. head over heels in love
5. I'm on your side
6. light at the end of the tunnel

page 9
1. spring to mind
2. off the cuff
3. double duty
4. time after time
5. beat around the bush
6. hit the brakes

page 10
1. tough break
2. turn up the heat
3. bite the hand that feeds you
4. feeling under the weather
5. stickup
6. within reason

page 11
1. inside out
2. for old times' sake
3. up to scratch
4. head in the clouds
5. line your pockets
6. second to none

page 12
1. shape up
2. knots in your stomach
3. lost in the shuffle
4. fooling around
5. cut a rug
6. fair and square

page 13
1. in the eyes of the law
2. bird's eye view
3. kick the habit
4. sell out
5. on the tip of your tongue
6. holy cow

page 14
1. scale down
2. on the same page
3. fire with both barrels
4. a tough nut to crack
5. tow the line
6. two peas in a pod

page 15
1. ace in the hole
2. rake over the coals
3. par for the course
4. time out
5. round trip
6. hole in one

page 16
1. see eye to eye
2. right up your alley
3. take your life into your hands
4. cut the mustard
5. a needle in a haystack
6. add insult to injury

PUZZLE ANSWERS pages 17 – 30

page 17
1. seventh heaven
2. time is money
3. share and share alike
4. hanging around
5. caught in the act
6. fall apart

page 18
1. sign on the dotted line
2. fly on the wall
3. the inside track
4. bite the bullet
5. sleep over
6. go down in history

page 19
1. fed up
2. one track mind
3. kick the bucket
4. say when
5. the last laugh
6. hit the ground running

page 20
1. over the moon
2. open arms
3. pull on your heartstrings
4. head to head
5. under fire
6. shake your head

page 21
1. raise some eyebrows
2. roll up your sleeves
3. follow in your footsteps
4. right off the bat
5. circle the wagons
6. long underwear

page 22
1. wear your heart on your sleeve
2. get it through your thick head
3. think positive
4. cross purposes
5. open the floodgates
6. down the road

page 23
1. off the deep end
2. in the nick of time
3. follow your nose
4. laugh all the way to the bank
5. one foot in the grave
6. winding down

page 24
1. cross the line
2. rain on your parade
3. hang on every word
4. a work in progress
5. pay up
6. a grain of truth

page 25
1. go from bad to worse
2. it crossed my mind
3. make a mountain out of a molehill
4. up to speed
5. a pain in the neck
6. a piece of cake

page 26
1. back flip
2. roll down the aisles
3. all in the imagination
4. in one ear, out the other
5. shoot the breeze
6. the underdog

page 27
1. get off your high horse
2. I've had it up to here
3. break your word
4. under the influence
5. high on the hog
6. double take

page 28
1. go into a tailspin
2. the crack of dawn
3. running on empty
4. sweep you off your feet
5. swear on a stack of bibles
6. knock-down, drag-out fight

page 29
1. in the right place at the right time
2. a feather in your cap
3. make a beeline
4. out of practice
5. look high and low
6. tip your hat

page 30
1. experience under your belt
2. up in the air
3. out of left field
4. a price on his head
5. much ado about nothing
6. get a handle on the situation

PUZZLE ANSWERS pages 31 – 44

page 31
1. a slap on the wrist
2. double over
3. hand me down
4. nose in the air
5. rough time
6. sing your praises

page 32
1. have it both ways
2. put your best foot forward
3. once upon a time
4. chicken out
5. man overboard
6. nose around

page 33
1. up to par
2. first and foremost
3. walk on air
4. half the battle
5. go the extra mile
6. out of hand

page 34
1. breaking news
2. kid around
3. upper crust
4. a month of Sundays
5. wide open
6. 5 o'clock shadow

page 35
1. it's for the best
2. stand out
3. lay down the law
4. spill the beans
5. tip your hand
6. in a bind

page 36
1. turn the tide
2. put two and two together
3. bend over backwards
4. you can count on me
5. hot off the press
6. fall down

page 37
1. the man on the street
2. read between the lines
3. two thumbs up
4. a monkey on your back
5. right on the money
6. the beginning of the end

page 38
1. turn over a new leaf
2. in the same boat
3. look down on him
4. in the back of your mind
5. where there's a will there's a way
6. tighten your belt

page 39
1. pick your brain
2. roadblock
3. two of a kind
4. cut from the same cloth
5. in short order
6. head and shoulders above the rest

page 40
1. turn the tables
2. the last straw
3. hit between the eyes
4. come full circle
5. pass the hat
6. turn back time

page 41
1. your eyes are bigger than your stomach
2. split the difference
3. back down
4. on the right track
5. take the bull by the horns
6. in your right mind

page 42
1. no strings attached
2. sit on the sidelines
3. trail off
4. moving up in the world
5. two sides of the same coin
6. sit up

page 43
1. be on the safe side
2. rock the boat
3. cross swords
4. time flies
5. draw the line
6. jump at the chance

page 44
1. mix business with pleasure
2. strike a chord
3. he's climbing the walls
4. the short end of the stick
5. I'm all ears
6. for once in your life

PUZZLE ANSWERS pages 45 – 52

page 45
1. 6 of one, half dozen of the other
2. meet you halfway
3. an open mind
4. still water runs deep
5. a match made in heaven
6. reflecting pool

page 46
1. wide awake
2. for days on end
3. running neck and neck
4. join hands
5. a meeting of the minds
6. half a chance

page 47
1. a clear conscience
2. one step forward, two steps back
3. the bottom line
4. keep your ear to the ground
5. change horses in mid-stream
6. under certain circumstances

page 48
1. scratch the surface
2. all thumbs
3. wear out your welcome
4. off the mark
5. get in shape
6. everything is under control

page 49
1. turn my back on you
2. day in, day out
3. a chip on your shoulder
4. the end of the road
5. back off
6. in the palm of your hand

page 50
1. at the last minute
2. put forth
3. at the eleventh hour
4. walk a thin line
5. stars in your eyes
6. a diamond in the rough

page 51
1. the bottom of my heart
2. flat broke
3. open and above board
4. above and beyond
5. the odds are stacked against us
6. close range

page 52
1. put the cart before the horse
2. an open and shut case
3. break even
4. count your blessings
5. a fish out of water
6. burn your bridges